To Doreen
with best wishes
John Muter
21 Dec 01

BATTLES AND MAJOR SKIRMISHES IN GREAT BRITAIN AND BRITISH WATERS 55BC - 1797

JOHN MUTER

ISBN 09537203 1 4

1

Battles & Major Skirmishes in Great Britain and British Waters 55BC - 1797

We now regard a battle as being combat, especially between large organised forces, but the meaning of the word has changed over the years as it used to be one of the groupings into which medieval armies were often divided. Such an army would normally, but not always, be formed into three Battles for ease of movement and control, and to facilitate tactical deployment. The first would be the Vanguard, the second the main Battle, and the third the Rearguard.

And what of an Army? A modern definition is an organised body of men armed for war, but the Laws of King Ine of Wessex (688 - 728) were quite specific, thus:

Up to seven men - Thieves
7 - 35 men   - A Band
36+   - An Army

It would appear, therefore, that some medieval battles could involve very few men, although this was not always the case, of course.

Some encounters in medieval times would not qualify as battles because of the numbers involved (when recorded) or in modern times because there was no engagement of major forces. It is in such instances that the word 'skirmish' is particularly appropriate, it being an irregular engagement between two small bodies of troops, especially detached or outlying parties of opposing armies.

Where it comes to dates, I hope that I have interpreted correctly the recognised inconsistencies in the Anglo-Saxon Chronicles. Where I have encountered conflicting dates recorded by later historians I have either recorded those on which the majority agree or recorded the options where none has agreed. Those recorded by Hardy in the margins of the Brut y Tywysogion have been quoted when it was found that other sources disagreed on the dates of battles in Wales.

I also found that some historians omitted from their accounts Constantine, who was King of the Picts from 789 until his death in 820. Others include him but style him as Constantine I with his namesakes, who were Kings of the Scots, as II (863 - 877), III (900 - 942), and IV (995 - 997).

Battles & Major Skirmishes
Waters 55t

I have followed this practice.
Despite my care, there may be err(
I am neither an historian, nor even a
that the compilation was made out of a
to trace such a list that already existe

It was an interesting exercise; almost every book in the bibliography provided at least one addition but, as comprehensive as it is, it is by no means definitive. How can it be when, for instance, the Rev Thomas Thomson in his 'A History of the Scottish People' (1895) writes that Robert the Bruce won 53 of his 70 battles, yet even he records only a handful?

There are certain to be other battles and skirmishes that are not mentioned here but that are known to some readers , and some will know details that are missing, but for now I am content to terminate my own research, as intriguing as it has been. I hope that the reader finds the results of interest.

Cumberland, England
John Muter
April 1999

Revised
March & Dec 2000
Feb & Mar 2001

BIBLIOGRAPHY

ANDERSON AO Early Sources of Scottish History 1922

AYRSHIRE ARCHEOLOGICAL & NATURAL HISTORY SOCIETY
2nd Series Vol 1 1950

AYRSHIRE ARCHEOLOGICAL & NATURAL HISTORY SOCIETY
2nd Series Vol 11 1976

BARRETT CRB Battles & Battlefields in England 1896

BARRON E M Scottish War of Independence 2nd Ed 1934

BARROW G W S Robert Bruce & the Community
of the Realm of Scotland 1965

BECKETT J V The East Midlands from AD1000 1988

BENNETT M The Civil Wars in Britain & Ireland 1638-51 1997

BLACK J B The Reign of Elizabeth 1558-1603 2nd Ed 1959

BROTCHIE T C F Battlefields of Scotland 1913

BRUCE G Paladin Dictionary of Battles 1986

BURNE AH More Battlefields of England 1952

CALDER J T Civil & Traditional History of Caithness 1887

CHALMERS G Caledonia 1887

CLARK G N The Later Stuarts 1660-1714 1934

CLARK KM Rye: A Short History 1991

COLLINGWOOD R G & MYRES J N L Roman Britain
& the English Settlements 2nd Ed 1937

DAVIES G The Early Stuarts 1603-60 2nd Ed 1959

DAVIES J A History of Wales 1993

DUNCAN A A M Scotland, The Making of the Kingdom 1975

ELLIS P Caesar's Invasion of Britain 1978

FALKUS M & GILLINGHAM J Historical Atlas of Britain 1981

FISHER D J V The Anglo Saxon Age 1973

GARMONSWAY G N Anglo Saxon Chronicles 2nd Ed 1954

GRANT A New History of Scotland - Independence & Nationhood 1984

GRAY J Sutherland and Caithness in Saga Time 1922

HARDY T D Monumenta Historica Britannica 1848 (including,
inter alia, the Brut y Tywysogion or The Chronicle of the Princes of Wales,
and the Annales Cambriae).

INVERNESS FIELD CLUB Middle Ages in the Highlands c1981

JACOB E F The Fifteenth Century 1399-1485 1961

KINROSS J The Battlefields of Britain 1979

LLOYD Sir J E History of Wales Part 1 3rd Ed 1939

LOCKYER R Tudor & Stuart Britain 1471-1714 1964

MACKENZIE A M Rise of the Stuarts 1935

MACKENZIE Rev W History of Galloway 1841

MACKIE J D The Earlier Tudors 1485-1558 1952

MACKIE R L Scotland 1916

Bibliography

MALORY Sir T Tales of King Arthur (Edited by Michael Senior 1980)

MARREN P Grampian Battlefields 1990

MARSH H Dark Age Britain 1970

MATTHEWS, C & J Arthurian Book of Days 1990

McKISACK M The Fourteenth Century 1307-1399 1959

McNEILL P & NICHOLSON R Historical Atlas of Scotland
c400-c1600 1975

MITCHELL D History of the Highlands & Gaelic Scotland 1900

OMAND D The Caithness Book 1972

PALMER A & V The Chronology of British History 1992

PATON J Scottish History & Life 1902

PETERS E Strongholds & Sanctuaries 1993

PINKERTON J An Enquiry into the History of Scotland 1814

POOLE A L From Domesday Book to Magna Carta 2nd Ed 1955

POWICKE Sir M The Thirteenth Century 1953

SADLER J Scottish Battles 1996

SALE R Owain Glyndwr's Way 1985

SCOTT R McN Robert Bruce, King of Scots 1982

SEYMOUR W Battles in Britain 1066-1547 (Vol 1) & 1642-1746
(Vol 2) 1975

SIZE N The Secret Valley 7th Ed 1996

SKENE W Celtic Scotland - History of Ancient Alban 2nd Ed 1886

SMURTHWAITE D Battlefields of Britain 1984

STENTON Sir F Anglo Saxon England 3rd Ed 1971

STEVENSON W Kirk & Parish of Auchtertool 1908

THOMSON Rev T A History of the Scottish People 1895

TRANTER N The Story of Scotland 1987

TREHARNE R & FULLARD H Muir's Historical Atlas 6th Ed 1963

WARNER D British Battlefields: The North (1972) Scotland &
The Borders (1975)

WILLIAMS B The Whig Supremacy 1714-1760 2nd Ed 1962

Battle List
The list provides only the basic details of each encounter and is in the following order:

Date; Place or Name (including alternative spellings)
Location
Opponents and result.

BC55 (25 Aug) Walmer/Deal
Kent
Julius Caesar bt Britons

BC54 (7 July) Bigbury
Devon
Julius Caesar bt Britons

BC54 South of R Thames
nr Brentford, Middx
Julius Caesar bt Cassivellaunus

BC54 (5 Aug) Wheathampstead
Herts
Julius Caesar bt Cassivellaunus

43 (by May) Medway
East Kent
Aulus Plautius bt Caratacus &
Togodumnus

43 (Aug/Sep) Colchester
Essex
Emperor Claudius bt Britons

51 Cefn Carnedd
6m ne Llanidloes, Monts
Publius Ostorius Scapula bt
Caratacus(Caradoc)
Note: Burne favours Black Hill/Clunbury
Hill ridge 1m s Purslow, Salop

61 Beaumaris
Anglesey - battle extended to Port
Dinorwic nr Caernarfon
Gaius Suetonius Paulinus bt Druids

61 Colchester
Essex
Boudicca (Boadicea) bt Quintus
Petillius Cerialis

61 Mancetter
se Atherstone, Warks
Gaius Suetonius Paulinus bt
Boudicca

83 Not recorded
N of Firth of Forth
Gnaeus Julius Agricola bt Picts

84 Mons Graupius
possibly Bennachie nr Inverurie,
Aberdeens
Gnaeus Julius Agricola bt Calgacus

183 Hadrian's Wall
Not known
Ulpius Marcellus bt Tribes of
Central Scotland

296 Silchester
Hants
Asclepiodotus & Constantius
Chlorus bt Allectus

Battle List

c384 River Cree
nr Newton Stewart, Wigtowns
Romans (Magnus Maximus) &
Picts bt Scots (Eugenius)

c384 River Doon
Kyle, Ayrs
Romans (Magnus Maximus) bt
Scots (Eugenius)

430 Not recorded
Not recorded
Germanus, Bishop of Auxerre, and
Britons bt Picts and Saxons

455 AEgelsthrep
Unidentified, possibly Aylesford,
Kent
Hengist & Horsa bt Vortigern, King
of a district in Wales

465 Wippedes fleot
Unidentified (possibly
Ebbsfleet,Kent)
Hengist & AEsc (later King of Kent))
bt Welsh

456-7 Creacanford/Crecgan ford
Unidentified, possibly Crayford,
Kent
Hengist & AEsc bt Vortigern

473 Not known
Not known
Hengist & AEsc bt Welsh

477 Cymenes ora
The Owers, s of Selsey Bill,
Sussex, now covered by the sea
AElle, King of Sussex, Cymen,
Wlencing, and Cissa (his sons) bt
Welsh

485 Mearcraedes burna
Not known
AElle, King of Sussex, bt Welsh

491 Andredes cester
Anderida, adj Pevensey, Sussex
AElle, King of Sussex, & Cissa bt
Britons

495 Cerdices ora
Unidentified
Cerdic, King of Wessex, & Cynric,
King of West Saxons, bt Welsh

5th Century Caledonian Forest
Unidentified
Arthur bt Saxons

500 or 517 Badon (Mons
Badonicus)
Possibly Bath, Somerset, or
Badbury, 5m se Swindon, Wilts
Arthur bt AElle, King of Sussex

508 Natan leag
Netley Marsh, Hants
Cerdic, King of Wessex, & Cynric,
King of West Saxons, bt Natanleod

514 Cerdices ora
Unidentified
Stuf & Wihtgar (West Saxons) bt
Britons

519 Cerdices ford
Unidentified
Cerdic, King of Wessex, & Cynric,
King of Saxons, bt Britons

527 Cerdices leag/Certicesford
Unidentified
Cerdic, King of Wessex, & Cynric,
King of Saxons, bt Britons

7

Battle List

530 Wihtgaraesburh
Isle of Wight
Cerdic, King of Wessex, & Cynric,
King of Saxons, bt Britons

537 (10 May) Dover
Kent
Arthur bt Mordred

537 (12 May) Barham Down
Kent. Midway between Dover &
Canterbury
Arthur bt Mordred

537 (Monday after Trinity Sunday)
Camlann
nr Salisbury, Wilts
Arthur bt Mordred

Notes on the battles of 537AD: The
Anglo-Saxon Chronicles provide the
year of the Battle of Camlann. It
can be deduced from Sir Thos
Malory that the battles at Dover and
Barham Down occurred in the same
year. He also provides the dates
for all three although C & J
Matthews' text suggests that the
battle at Camlann took place during
the winter. Malory identifies
Camlann as being near Salisbury .
In view of the locations and dates of
both preceding battles and that
Mordred drew his forces from
around London, this seems more
likely than Birdoswald (6m nw
Brampton) or Bewcastle (9m nnw
Brampton), Cumberland, as
suggested by another source.

542 Glen Water
Confluence of Glen Water & R Irvine,
Ayrs
King Arthur bt ?

552 Searoburh
Old Sarum, Wilts
Cynric, King of W Saxons, bt
Britons/Welsh

556 Beranburh
Barbury Castle, 6m s Swindon,
Wilts
Cynric, King of W Saxons, &
Ceawlin, King of Wessex, bt Britons

568 Wibbandun
Unidentified
Ceawlin, King of Wessex, & Cutha
(W Saxon) bt AEthelberht, King of
Kent

571 Bedcanford
Unidentified, but presumed n of
Luton, Beds and poss. Aylesbury,
Bucks
Cuthwulf (W Saxon) bt Britons

573 Lora/Delgu/Telocho
Kintyre
Picts bt Duncath MacConail
MacCongail

573 Arderydd/Armterid/Atterith
Arthuret 1m s Longtown,
Cumberland
Rhydderch ap Tudwal bt
Gwenddolen ap Ceidio (Victor also
recorded as Elifer)

577 Deorham
Dyrham/Hinton Hill, Glos. 7m n
Bath, Som.
Cuthwine (W Saxon) & Ceawlin,
King of Wessex, bt Conmail,
Condidan, and Forinmail (British
Kings)

577 Metcaud
Lindisfarne, North'd
Urien(Urbgen) King of Reged fought
Deodric, King of Bernicia. Result
not known. Possibly identical with:

6th Century Argoed Llwyfain
Unidentified
Owain of Reged bt Angles under
the Prince of Fflamddwyn

578 Isle of Jura
Argyll
Possibly Scots v Britons

584 Fethan leag
Stoke Lyne ne Oxon
Ceawlin, King of Wessex, & Cutha
(W Saxon) bt Britons

590 Leithreid
Sutherland
Aidan, King of Dalriada bt ?

592 Adam's Grove
Alton Priors, Wilts
? bt Ceawlin, King of Wessex .

593 Woddesbeorg/Wodnesbeorg
Woodborough, Wilts
? bt Ceawlin, King of Wessex,
Cwichelm (W Saxon) & Crida

593-600 Catraeth
Poss. Catterick, Yorks
? bt Owain (Recorded in the
"Gododdin" of Aneirin)

596 Ratho
8m wsw Edinburgh
Aidan, King of Dalriada bt ?

596 Ardsendoin (Miathi)
poss. Dumyat, Clackmannan, or
Inverarity, Angus
Aidan, King of Dalriada bt the Miathi

598 Chirchind/Kirkinn
Angus/Kincardineshire
Picts bt Cumbrians & Aiden, King of
Dalriada

c600 Corinnie
Aberdeenshire
Picts bt Aidan, King of Dalriada

603 Daegsenstan
Poss. Dawston in Liddesdale,
Roxburghs
AEthelfrith, King of N'bria bt Aiden,
King of Dalriada

605-6 Chester
Cheshire
AEthelfrith, King of N'bria bt Welsh,
led by Brocmail

607 Unidentified
Not known
Ceolwulf, King of W Saxons bt
South Saxons

Battle List

613-6 Cair Legion (Chester)
Cheshire
AEthelfrith, King of N'bria bt Selyf
ap Cynau (Solomon, son of Cynan,
King of Powys) & Cadwol Crisban.

614 Beandun
Bindon, nr Axmouth, Devon
Cynegils, King of Wessex, &
Cwichelm, his son bt Welsh

616 (17 Apr) Eigg, Isle of
Inverness
Pirates bt Donnan

617 River Idle
nr Bawtry, Yorks
Raedwald, King of E Anglia bt
AEthelfrith, King of N'bria

621 Cindelgthen
Loch Fyne, Argyll
Conal MacSuibne bt Conaing

627 Ardacorain
Kintyre
Conadh Kerr,King of Dalriada bt
Fiachna MacDemain

628 Cirencester
Glos
Penda, King of Mercia bt Cynegils,
King of Wessex, & Cwichelm, his
son

629 Faedhaeoin
Scotland
Rigullan bt Conadh Kerr, King of
Dalriada

c630 River Severn (banks of)
Glos
? bt Idris of Merioneth

630 Meicaren
Unidentified
Catguallaun bt Etguin

633 (14 Oct) Haethfelth
Hatfield Chase, nr Doncaster, Yorks
Penda, King of Mercia, &
Cadwallon, King of Gwynedd, bt
Edwin, King of N'bria

634 York
Cadwallon, King of Gwynedd, bt
Osric, King of Deira

634 Heavenfield/Denisesburna
Rowley Burn, s of Hexham, N'land
Oswald, King of N'bria bt
Cadwallon, King of Gwynedd

634 Calathros
Callander, Stirlings
Oswald, King of N'bria bt Donald
Brecc, King of Dalriada

635 Seguise
Dalguise, nr Dunkeld, Perths
Garnait bt Family of Nectan

641 (5Aug) Maserfelth
Poss.Oswestry(Cogwy/Cocboy),
Salop
Penda, King of Mercia bt Oswald,
King of N'bria

642 (Dec) Strathcarron
R. Carron, Stirlings
Owain of Strathclyde bt Donald
Brecc, King of Dalriada

Battle List

652 Bradenforda
Bradford on Avon, Wilts
Cenwalh, King of Wessex, bt
Britons

655 Winwidfeld
R, Winwald, nr Leeds, Yorks
Oswiu, King of Bernicia bt Penda,
King of Mercia

658 Peonnan/Penselwood
Pinhoe, 7m nw Exeter, Devon
Cenwalh, King of Wessex bt Welsh

661 (Easter) Posentesburh
Posbury, Devon
Cenwalh, King of Wessex, bt
Britons

665 Badon (Mons Badonicus)
Poss. Bath, Somerset, or Badbury,
5m se Swindon, Wilts
Britons v English (Opponents and
result not recorded)

674 Not recorded
Northumbria
Ecgfrith, King of N'bria bt Wulfhere,
King of Mercia

675 Biedanheafod
nr Marlborough, Wilts
Wulfhere, King of Mercia v
AEscwine, King of Wessex (Result
not recorded)

676 Rochester
Kent
AEthelred, King of Mercia bt Locals

679 Trent
Notts
AEthelred, King of Mercia, bt
Ecgfrith, King of N'bria

682 Not recorded
Not recorded
Centwine, King of Wessex, bt
Britons

683 Glenmairison
Mureston Water, West Lothian;
joins R Almond at West Calder
Donald Brec, King of Dalriada bt
Domnal Brec Aedan and Angles

685 (20 May) Dunnichen Moss /
Nechtanesmere
Dunnichen-Letham, between Forfar
& Arbroath, Angus
Brude MacBeli, King of Picts, bt
Ecgfrith, King of N'bria

686 Kent/Isle of Wight (Records
conflict)
Not recorded
Caedwalla, King of Wessex, & Mul
bt Locals

c 704 Valley of the Leven
Dunbs
Britons bt Men of Dalriada

710 R. Tamar (west of)
Cornwall
Ine, King of Wessex, bt Geraint, King
of Britons (of Cornwall)

710 Between Haefe & Caere
Between R. Avon, Linlithgow,
W Lothian & R Carron, Stirlings
Beorhtfrith bt Picts

Battle List

711 Mano
Clackmannans
Saxons bt Picts

711 Loch Arklet
2m e Inversnaid, Stirlings
Scots bt Britons

715 Adam's Grove
Alton Priors, Wilts
Ceolred, King of Mercia bt Ine, King
of Wessex

717 Minvircc
Glenfalloch, Perths
Scots bt Britons

719 Finglen
Braes of Lorn, n shore of Loch
Tralaig, Argyll
Selbach, King of Dalriada bt
Ainbhceallach

719 (6 Oct) Ardde-anesbi
off Kintyre (at sea)
Duncan Bec bt Selbach, King of
Dalriada

721 Garth Maelog
nr Llanbister, Radnors or Ruthyn,
Glam
Welsh bt English

721 Pencon/Pencoed
nr Bridgend, Glam
Welsh bt English

722 R Hayle (estuary)
Cornwall
Ine, King of Wessex bt S Saxons

722 Taunton
Somerset
AEthelburg of N'bria bt Ealdberht,
Prince of Wessex

725 Unidentified
Not known
Ine, King of Wessex bt S Saxons

727 Irroisfoichnae
Ross-Feochan, nr Loch Awe, Argyll
Selbach bt Eochach

727 Fortriu/Fortren
Southern Strathearn, Perths,
betwen Rivers Almond & Teith
Angus, King of Fortriu bt Drust, King
of Picts three times.

727-9 Monacrib/Crei/Moncreiffe Hill
3m se Perth, Perths
Ungust (Angus) bt Elpin (Alpin),
King of Picts

728 Caislen Crathi/Crede Castle
nr Scone, Perths
Nechtan bt Alpin, King of Picts

728-30 Monticarno
nr Loch Inch, Speyside, Moray
Ungust (Angus) bt Nechtan, King of
Picts

729-30 (12 Aug) Dromaderg
Blathug/Blathmig
1m w Bellaty, Angus
Ungust (Angus) bt Drust, King of Picts

733 Somerton
Somerset
AEthelbald, King of Mercia bt
AEthelheard, King of Wessex

Battle List

734 Not recorded
Scotland
Brud, King of Picts bt Talorgan

736 Cnuicc Coirpri (cf 739 Twini
Onirbre)
Scotland
Talorgan bt Muredhach

737 Not recorded
Scotland
Brother (not recorded) bt Talorgan

739 Dalriada
Scotland
Ungust (Angus), King of Picts bt
Dungal & Ferach

739 Twini Onirbre (cf 736 Cnuicc
Coirpri)
Scotland
Talorgan bt Murdac

c740 Forboros
poss. Forres, Moray
Picts of Moray bt Scots of Dalriada

742 Dunadd (cf 743 Droma
Cathvaoil)
Poss. Dunnet, Caithness
Oengus MacFergus bt Scots

743 Droma Cathvaoil (cf 742
Dunadd)
Scotland
Ungust (Angus), King of Picts bt
Dalriads

744 Mugdock
Dunbartons
Angus, King of Picts bt Britons

750 Maes y dawc/Catho/Moce-
tauc/Metgadawc
poss Mugdock, Dunbartons
Welsh of Strathclyde bt Picts
(Talorgan)

752 Beorgfeord
Burford, Oxon
Cuthred, King of Wessex bt
AEthelbald, King of Mercia

752 Sreith
Strath in The Mearns, Kincardines
Between Picts

756 Alcluith
Dumbarton
Eadberht, King of N'bria & Angus,
King of Picts bt Britons of
Strathclyde

757 Merantun
Marden, Wilts
Cyneheard, Prince of Wessex bt
Cynewulf, King of Wessex

760 Hereford
Hereford
English v Welsh (result unknown)

761 (6 Aug) AEdwiresclif
Unidentified
Moll, King of N'bria bt Oswine, King
of Deira

768 Fortren/Fortriu
Southern Strathearn, Perths,
between Rivers Almond and Teith
Picts (Kenneth/Ciniod) bt Aed Find,
King of Dalriada

13

Battle List

771 Hastings
Sussex
Offa, King of Mercia, bt Locals

776 Otford
Kent
Kentishmen bt Offa, King of Mercia

779 Benson
Oxon
Offa, King of Mercia bt Cynewulf,
King of Wessex

788 Not recorded
Scotland
Constantine I bt Conal MacTeige,
King of Picts

793 (8 Jun) Lindisfarne
Northumberland
Danes bt Locals

796 Rhuddlan
Denbighs
Cenwulf bt Offa, King of Mercia

798 Romney Marsh
Kent
Ceolwulf, King of Mercia bt
Eadberht Praen, King of Kent

798 (2Apr) Whalley
Lancs
? bt Alric son of Heardberht

798 Not recorded
Unidentified
? bt Caradoc

Between 801 - 1199 Lendrun
("Bloody Butts")
3$\frac{1}{2}$m se Turriff, Aberdeens
Locals v Danes. Result not recorded

802 Kempsford
Glos
Weohsten of Wiltshire bt
AEthelmund of Wessex

812 Not Recorded
Cambria
Howel bt Cynan

815 Not Known
Anglesey
Howel bt Cynan

816 Not Known
Anglesey
Cynan bt Howel

818 Llanmais/Llanvaes
nr Beaumaris, Anglesey
Not recorded

822 Deganwy
Caerns
Mercians bt Welsh

825 Galford
Cornwall
Men of Devon bt Britons (of
Cornwall)

825 Ellandun
Poss. Wroughton, Wilts
Egbert, King of Wessex bt
Beornwulf, King of Mercia

14

Battle List

825 Not Recorded
North of R Thames
AEthelwulf, son of Egbert, King of
Wessex bt Baldred, King of Kent

829 Not Recorded
Mercia
Egbert, King of Wessex bt Ludeca,
King of Mercia

836 Laicht Castle
2m nnw Dalmellington, Ayrs
Picts bt Alpin, King of Dalriada

836 Carhampton
Somerset
Danes bt Egbert, King of Wessex

838 Hingston Down
West of lower R Tamar, Cornwall
Egbert, King of Wessex & Mercia bt
Britons & Danes

839 Fortriu
Southern Strathearn, Perths,
between Rivers Almond and Teith
Danes bt Picts & Scots

839 Not Recorded
Not Recorded
Danes bt Eogan

840 Southampton
Hants
Ealdorman Wulfheard bt Danes

840 Portland
Dorset
Danes bt AEthelhelm, Ealdorman of
Dorset

843 Carhampton
Somerset
Danes bt AEthelwulf, King of
Wessex

844 Cyveiliog
Monts
Not recorded

848 Finnant
Cambria
Not recorded

848 River Parrett
Somerset
Eanwulf, Ealdorman of Somerset &
Dorset bt Danes

850 Wiceganbeorg
Not Recorded
Ealdorman Ceorl bt Danes

851 Canterbury & London
Kent & London
Danes bt Beornwulf, King of Mercia

851 Aclea
prob. Oakley, n.Sandwich, e Great
Stonar, Kent
AEthelwulf, King of Wessex bt
Danes

851 Off Sandwich
Kent
Aethelstan, King of Kent bt Danes

853 Thanet
Kent
Danes bt Ealdorman Ealhere &
Kentishmen, and Huda &
Surreymen

Battle List

855 Not recorded
Not recorded
Rhodri ap Merfyn ("The Great") bt
Danes (Hofn)

860 Winchester
Hants
Ealdorman Osric & Hants men, and
Ealdorman Aethelwulf & Berks men
bt Danes

862 Gweithen
Cambria
Cadweithen bt ?

866 Fortrenn
Southern Strathearn, Perths,
between Rivers Almond and Teith
Olaf, King of Dublin bt Picts

866 (1 Nov) York
Hingwar bt Locals

867 (21 Mar) York
Danes bt AElle, King of
Northumbria & Osbert, his
predecessor

869 Cryn Onan ("Ash Hill")
Cambria
Not recorded

869 (20 Nov)Thetford (site also
recorded as Hoxne, Suffolk) Norfolk
Ivar bt Edmund, King of East Anglia

870 Dumbarton
Dunbs
Olaf, King of Dublin bt Locals

870 (31 Dec) Englefield
Berks
Ealdorman AEthelwulf bt Danes

871 (4 Jan) Reading
Berks
Danes bt AEthelred, King of
Wessex & Alfred, his brother

871 (8 Jan) Ashdown
Lowbury Hill nw Streatley, Berks
Aethelred, King of Wessex & Alfred,
his brother bt Bagsac (Bag Secg),
King of Danes

871 (22 Jan) Basing
sw Reading, Berks
Danes bt AEthelred, King of
Wessex & Alfred, his brother

871 (March) Meretun/Merantun
Marden 9m sw Marlborough, Wilts
Danes bt AEthelred, King of
Wessex & Alfred, his brother

871 (May) Wilton
Wilts
Danes bt Alfred, King of Wessex

873 Menegyd
Anglesey
Not recorded

873 Bangolen
Not recorded
? bt Cynan

874 Repton
(poss) Derbys
Danes bt Burgred, King of Mercia

875 Dollar
Clackmannan
Thorsten bt Constantine II, King of
the Scots

Battle List

876 Carlisle
Cumberland
Norwegians & Danes under Halfdan
bt Angles

876 Wareham
Dorset
Alfred, King of Wessex bt Danes

877 Not Recorded
Anglesey
Danes bt Rhodri Mawr, King of
Powys & Gwynedd

877 Crail
Fife
Danes bt Constantine II, King of the
Scots

877 Dollar,
Clackmannan
Danes bt Constantine II, King of the
Scots

877 Inverdovet/Black Cave
1m e Newport on Tay, Fife
Danes bt Constantine II, King of the
Scots

877 Exeter
Devon
Guthrum bt Men of Wessex

878 (Jan) Not Recorded
nr Chippenham, Wilts
Danes (Guthrum) bt Alfred, King of
Wessex

878 (Easter) Cynwit
Countisbury Hill, Devon
Alfred, King of Wessex bt Danes

878 (11-12 May) Ethandun
Edington, Wilts
Alfred, King of Wessex bt Danes
(Guthrum)

881 Conway (mouth of)
Caerns
Anarawd, son of Rhodri Mawr, King
of Powys & Gwynedd bt AEthelred,
King of Mercia

885 Rochester
Kent
Alfred, King of Wessex bt Danes

886 London
Alfred, King of Wessex bt Danish
supporters

893 Farnham
Bucks
Alfred, King of Wessex bt Danes

893 Bleamfleote
Benfleet, Essex
Alfred, King of Wessex bt Danes
(Haesten)

893 Buttington on Severn
nr Welshpool, Powys
Alfred, King of Wessex (forces) &
Welsh bt Danes

893 Chester
Cheshire
Alfred, King of Wessex (forces) bt
Danes

894 Chichester
Sussex
English bt Danes

Battle List

895 River Lea
Not recorded, prob Essex, ne London
Danes bt Alfred, King of Wessex (forces)

896 Uncertain
poss Poole Harbour, Dorset
English bt Danes

900 Penros
Ros Meilon, nr Holyhead, Anglesey
Igmond bt ?

900 Dunnottar
2m s Stonehaven, Kincardines
Danes bt Donald II, King of the Scots

902/4 The Holm
Not Recorded
Danes bt Edward the Elder, King of Wessex

903 Dunkeld
Perths
Danes bt Constantine III, King of the Scots

904 Dinerth
Llandabarn vach, Cardigans
Danes bt Maelog Claudus

904 Forteviot
Strathearn sw Perth, Perths
Constantine III, King of the Scots bt Danes

904(?) Scone
Perths
Constantine III, King of the Scots bt Danes

910 (6 Aug) Tettenhall
nr Wednesfield 3m e Tettenhall, Staffs
Edward the Elder, King of Wessex bt Halfdan II & Eowils

914/918 Corbridge
Northumberland
Ragnall of York bt Constantine III, King of the Scots

914/6 Hook Norton
Oxon
Danes bt Locals

914/6 Luton
Beds
Locals bt Danes

915/7 Archenfield
Herefords/Glos border
Men of Herefordshire & Gloucestershire bt Danes

916 (19 Jan) Brecenanmere
Llangorse Lake nr Brecon, Brecknock
AEthelflaed, "Lady of the Mercians" bt Welsh

917 (July) Derby
Derbys
AEthelflaed, "Lady of the Mercians" bt Danes

919 Dynas Newydd
Cambria
Not recorded

Battle List

920 Between Tempsford & Bedford
Beds
Bedford Garrison bt Danes

920 Wigingamere
Not Recorded
English bt Danes

920 (summer) Tempsford
Beds
English bt Danes

920 (autumn) Colchester
Essex
English bt Danes

920 (autumn) Maldon
Essex
English bt Danes

920 Davenport
Lancs
Edward the Elder, King of Wessex
bt Danes

921 Tinmore/Tynemoore
prob. Northumberland
Constantine III, King of the Scots bt
Danes

923 York
Ragnald bt Locals

937 Brunanburh
Uncertain but poss Bromborough,
10m n Chester, Cheshire
Athelstan, King of Wessex &
Mercia bt Danes (Olaf) &
Constantine III, King of the Scots
Note: Burne favours Brinsworth,
Yorks

c940 Dunmail Raise
between Grasmere & Thirlmere,
Cumberland/Westmorland border
Edmund, King of England bt
Dunmail, King of Strathclyde &
Cumbria

941 Tyninghame
1½m ne East Linton/4½m w Dunbar,
East Lothian
Danes bt Edmund, King of Saxons
(forces)

942 Not Recorded
Edmund, King of Saxons bt Idwal
Foel ap Anarawd

943 Tamworth
Staffs
Danes (Olaf) bt English

948 Castleford
Yorks
Danes bt Eadred, King of Wessex

950 Nant Carno
6m nw Caerws, Powys
Iago & Idwal bt sons of Hywel the
Good

950 Dale/The Dales
On R Thurso, 1m se Westerdale,
Caithness
Liot bt Skuli

953 "Bloody Pots" (see also 1001-
1010 Gardenstown)
nr Gamrie, Banffs
Locals bt Danes

Battle List

954 Fetteresso
2m w Stonehaven, Kincardines
Moray men bt Malcolm I, King of the
Scots

954 near Llanrwst
Caerns
Men of Gwynedd bt sons of Hywel
the Good

954/5 Steinmore
Stainmore, w Bowes Yorks
Earl Maccus bt Eric Bloodaxe, King
of York

961 Cullen ("The Bauds")
Moray
Indulf, King of the Scots bt Danes

965 Drumcrob/Crup
Dunning, Perths
Dubh (Duffus), King of the Scots bt
Cuilean

967 Forres (at the bridge of Kinloss)
Moray
Cullen bt Dubh (Duffus) to become
King of the Scots

971 Ybandonia
poss. Abington, Lanarks
Amderlh bt Cullen, King of the
Scots

971 Moss of the Corney
Abercorn, 3m w Queensferry,
W Lothian
Britons bt Kenneth, King of the Scots

973 Luncarty
n Perth, Perths
Kenneth II, King of the Scots, bt
Danes

977 Skida Moor/Skidmore
Caithness
Liotr bt Magbiodr (Earl MacBeth)

979 Hirbarth
Cambria
Howel, son of Ieuav bt Constantine,
son of Iago

980 Thanet
Kent
Not Recorded

980 Dungal's Noep
nr Duncansby, Caithness
Sigurd bt Hundi and Melsnati
Note: this battle is also placed at
Skitten Moor, nw Wlck. Cf Skida
Moor/Skidmore 977 & 995.

980/1 Southampton
Hants
"Pirates" (Danes?) bt Locals

981 Padstow
Cornwall
Not Recorded

981 Llanwenog
on R Teifi, nr Lampeter, Cardigans
Godfrey, son of Harold bt ?

982 Portland
Dorset
"Pirates" (Danes?) v Locals

Battle List

987 Anglesey
Not Recorded
Godfrey, son of Harold bt Welsh

987/8 Watchet
Somerset
? bt Goda of Devonshire

988 Maldon
Northey Island, Essex
Brihtnoth/Byhrtnoth, Ealdorman of
Essex bt Danes

991 (10 Aug) Maldon
Northey Island, Essex
Olaf Tryggvason, later King of
Norway bt Brihtnoth/Byhrtnoth,
Ealdorman of Essex

993 Bamburgh
Northumberland
Danes bt Locals

993 Llangwm
Denbighs
Sons of Meuruc bt Sons of
Maredudd

994 London
Londoners bt Olaf Tryggvason, King
of Norway & Swein, son of King of
Denmark

995 Skida Moor/Skidmore
Caithness
Earl Sigurd bt Findlay of Moray

997 Lydford
Devon
Danes bt Locals

997 Watchet
Somerset
Danes bt Locals

997 Rathinveramon
Fort at mouth of R Almond n Perth,
Perths
Kenneth III bt Constantine IV to
become King of the Scots

999 St David's
Pembrokes
Danes bt Maredudd

999 Rochester
Kent
Danes bt Locals

1001 AEthelingadene
Hants/Sussex Border
Danes bt Men of Hants

1001-1010 Gardenstown/Gamrie
Bay ("Bloody Pits")(see also 953
"Bloody Pots")
Banffs
Sheriff of Banff bt Danes

1001 Pinhoe
2m ne Exeter Devon
Danes bt Kola, King's High Reeve &
Ecdsige, King's Reeve

1004 Thetford
Norfolk
Danes (Swein, son of King of
Denmark) bt Ulfkell Snilling of
Norfolk

Battle List

1005 Monnivaird/Monzievaird
Strathearn, Perths
Malcolm II bt Kenneth III to become
King of the Scots

1006 East Kennet
5m w Marlborough, Wilts
Danes bt English

1006 Durham
Co. Durham
Uhtred of Durham bt Malcolm II,
King of the Scots

1008/9 Nairn
Nairns
Swein bt Malcolm II, King of the
Scots

1010 (5 May) Ringmere
Either Roudham Heath, 4m ne, or
Rymer 4m s Thetford, Norfolk
Danes (Thorkell the Tall &
Hemming) bt Ulfkell Snilling of
Norfolk

1010 Mortlach
³/₄ m s Dufftown, Moray
Malcolm II, King of the Scots bt
Danes (Swein)

1010 St Bride
Douglas, Lanarks
Malcolm II, King of the Scots bt
Danes

1010 Camuston
Poss. Camus Stone at Inverugie,
1m s Hopeman, Moray
Malcolm II, King of the Scots bt
Danes (Camus)

c1010 Cruden Bay
sw Peterhead, Aberdeens
Scots bt Danes

1010 Slains Castle
sw Peterhead, Aberdeens
Scots bt Danes

1010 Brechin
Fife
Scots bt Danes

1011 Canterbury
Kent
Olaf bt Locals

1013 London
Thorkell the Tall & King AEthelred II
bt Danes (King Swein)

1014 Lindsey
Lincs
Aethelred bt Danes

1016 Penselwood
Somerset
Danes (Cnut, son of Swein, King of
Denmark) v Edmund Ironside, King
of Wessex. Indecisive

1016 Sherston
Wilts
Danes (Cnut, son of Swein, King of
Denmark) v Edmund Ironside, King
of Wessex. Indecisive

1016 Brentford
Middx
Edmund Ironside, King of Wessex
bt Cnut, son of Swein, King of
Denmark

Battle List

1016 Otford
Kent
Edmund Ironside, King of Wessex
bt Cnut, son of Swein, King of
Denmark

1016 (18 Oct) Assandun
Ashingdon, 5m n Southend on Sea,
Essex
Cnut, son of Swein, King of
Denmark bt Edmund Ironside, King
of Wessex

1016 Coldstream
Berwicks
Not Recorded

1018 Carham on Tweed
nw Wark, Northumberland
Malcolm II, King of the Scots &
Owain the Bold, King of Strathclyde
bt Uhtred of Durham

1022 Abergwili
2m e Carmarthen, Carm
Llywelyn ap Seisyll bt Rnain

1032 Iratur/Hiraethwy/Traethwy
Cambria
Sons of Edwin v Sons of Ryderch.
Result not recorded

1034 Flanders Moss
w Causewayhead 2m n Stirling,
Stirlings
Cnut, King of Anglo Saxons v
Malcolm II, King of the Scots.
Result undecided

1034-40 Not Known
Not Known
Cnut, King of Anglo Saxons bt
Duncan I, King of the Scots

1039 Rhyd y Groes/Crosford
6m se Welshpool, Mont
Gruffydd ap Llywelyn, King of
Gwynedd & Powys bt Leofric, Earl
of Mercia

1039 Pen Cadeir
12m n Carmarthen, Carms
Gruffydd ap Llywelyn bt Howel,
Prince of Glamorgan

1040 Sandwick (south of) (naval)
Orkneys
Thorfinn bt Duncan I, King of the
Scots

1040 (14 Aug) Torfness
prob. Burghead, Moray
Thorfinn bt Duncan I, King of the
Scots

1040 (15 Aug) Elgin
Moray
MacBeth bt Duncan I to become
King of the Scots

1040 Thurso
Caithness
Thorkell bt Modden

1040 Pwll Dyvach
Dyfedd
Howel, Prince of Glamorgan bt
Danes

1042 Abertywi
s Carmarthen, Carms
Gruffydd ap Llywelyn bt Howel, son
of Edwin

Battle List

1046 Pentland Firth
off Rattar Brough, e Dunnet Head,
Caithness
Thorfinn bt Ragnvald (Ronald)

1049 (29 Jul) River Usk
South Wales
Danes & Gruffydd, King of
Gwynedd & Powys bt Locals

1052 (28 Jul) Menai Straits
Caerns
Guthorm bt Margad

1052 Porlock
Somerset
Earl Harold bt English

1053 Hereford
Herefords
AElfgar of Mercia & Gruffydd, King
of Gwynedd & Powys bt Earl Ralph

1054 River Earn
Confluence of Rivers Earn & Tay se
Perth, Perths
Earl Siward bt MacBeth, King of the
Scots

1056 Glasbury on Wye
Brecknock
Welsh bt Bishop of Hereford

1057 (24/27 Jul) Dunsinane Hill
("The Seven Sleepers")
Sidlaw Hills, ne Scone, Perths
Malcolm Canmore bt MacBeth, King
of the Scots

1057 (15 Aug) Lumphanan
Aberdeens
Malcolm Canmore, later Malcolm III
bt MacBeth, King of the Scots

1058 (17 Mar) Essie
Strathbogie, Aberdeens
Malcolm Canmore bt Lulach to
become Malcolm III, King of the
Scots

1063 (5 Aug) Snowdonia
Caerns
Harold Godwinson bt Gruffydd, King
of Gwynedd & Powys

1066 Lindsey
Lincs
Earl Edwin bt Tostig

1066 (20 Sep) Gate Fulford
Yorks
Harold Hardrada, King of Norway bt
Earls Morcar & Edwin

1066 (25 Sep) Stamford Bridge
Yorks
Harold II (Godwinson), King of
England bt Harold Hardrada, King
of Norway

1066 (14 Oct) Hastings
Telham Hill, Battle, Sussex
William, Duke of Normandy bt
Harold II (Godwinson) to become
King of England

1066 (Oct/Nov) Southwark
Surrey
English bt William I, King of
England

1069 Stafford
Staffs
William I, King of England bt
Mercians

Battle List

c1070 Ravenglass
Cumberland
William le Meschin bt Earl Boethar

c1070 Barnscar (since razed)
n Ravenglass, Cumberland.
William le Meschin bt Earl Boethar

c1070 Carlisle
Cumberland
Dolfin bt Ranulf Meschin, Earl of
Carlisle

1074/8 Goodwick Moor
1m nw Fishguard, Pembrokes
Trahaearn ap Caradog ap Edwyn
bt Rhys ap Owain

1081 Mynydd Carn
Poss. Mynydd Carn Goch, $\frac{1}{2}$m e
Gorseinon, Glam
Gruffydd ap Cynan bt Trahaearn ap
Caradog

1092 Grasmere
Westmorland
Earl Boethar bt William II, King of
England

1092 Carlisle
Cumberland
William II, King of England bt Dolfin

1093 (13 Nov) Alnwick
Northumberland
Robert, Earl of Northumbria bt
Malcolm III, King of the Scots

c1093 Hardknott Pass & Castle
Cumberland
Ranulf Meschin,Earl of Carlisle bt
Angles

c1093 Raven Howe
7m w Shap, Westmorland
Earl Ackin bt Ranulf Meschin, Earl
of Carlisle

1094 Not Recorded
Not Recorded
Duncan II temporarily deposed
Donald III to become King of the
Scots for less than a year

1097 Not Recorded
Not Recorded
Edgar Mac Malcolm bt Donald III to
become King of the Scots

1098 Menai Straits
Caerns
Magnus Barefoot, King of Norway
bt Earls of Chester & Shrewsbury

c1100 Newlands
On Buttermere - Keswick road,
Cumberland
Earl Boethar bt Ranulf Meschin,
Earl of Carlisle

c1105 Brackenthwaite
Cumberland
William Meschin bt Earl Boethar

c1105 Rannerdale
Cumberland
Earl Boethar bt William Meschin

1130 Inchbare
Stickatho/Stracathro
4m n Brechin, Angus
David I, King of the Scots bt Earl of
Moray

Battle List

1136 (1 Jan) Swansea
Glam
Welsh bt Anglo Norman colonists

1136 (26 Jun) Off Tankerness
Orkney
Earl Paul bt Olvi Riot

1136 (27 Jun) Yell Sound
Shetland
Earl Paul bt Earl Ragnvald (Ronald)

1136 Carlisle
Cumberland
David I, King of the Scots bt English

1138 Clitheroe
Lancs
William FitzDuncan bt English

1138 (16 Feb) Roxburgh
Roxburghs
David, King of the Scots bt
Stephen, King of England

1138 (22 Aug) "Battle of the Standard"
Cowton Moor, 3m n Northallerton,
Yorks
Northern Barons & Archbishop
Thurston of York bt David I, King of
the Scots

1141 (2 Feb) Lincoln
Lincs
Ranulf, Earl of Chester & Robert of
Gloucester bt Stephen, King of England

1141 (14 Sep) Winchester
Hants
Empress Matilda bt Queen Matilda

1143 Wilton
Wilts
King Stephen bt ?

1151/3
Aberdeen/Hartlepool/Whitby/Filey
Aberdeen/Co Durham/Yorks
Eystein, King of Norway bt Locals

1153 Tutbury
Staffs
Henry of Anjou's siege was
successful

1154 Thurso
Caithness
Eystein, King of Norway & Earl
Ragnvald bt Earl Harald

1156 (6 Jan) Isle of Islay
Argyll
Godfrey, King of Man & Hebrides v
Somerled, Lord of the Isles.
Inconclusive

1157/8 Murkfjord
Poss. Loch Glendhu, Sutherland
Sweyn bt Gilli Odran

1158 (24 Oct) Orkney
Svein and Erland bt Harald,
Earl of Orkney

1160 Not Recorded
Galloway
Malcolm IV, King of the Scots bt
Fergus

1164 The Knock ("Bloody Mire")
Between Renfrew & Paisley,
Renfrews
Walter Fitz Alan bt Somerled, Lord
of the Isles

Battle List

1173 Carlisle
Cumberland
Robert de Vaux bt William the Lion, King of the Scots

1174 (13 Jul) Alnwick
Northumberland
English bt William the Lion, King of the Scots

1185 (1 Jan) Not Recorded
Galloway
Roland bt Gilpatrick

1185 (30 Sep) Not Recorded
Galloway
Roland bt Gilcolm

1187 (31 Jul) Mamgarvia Moor
Speyside, Moray
Roland of Galloway bt Donald ban MacWilliam

1190 Cornaigmore ("Battle of the Sheaves")
Isle of Tiree, Argyll
Danes bt Locals

1194 Conway
Caerns
Llewellyn ap Gwynedd bt ?

1196 River Oykell
Sutherland/Ross
William the Lion, King of the Scots bt Earl Harold

1196 Clardon Hill
2m e Thurso, Caithness
Harold the Old bt Harold Ungi

1198/9 Dalharrold
Loch Naver, Sutherland
Ragnvald Gudrudson bt Harold Maddadson

1199 Mold
Flints
Llewellyn ap Gwynedd bt ?

1208/9 Skye
Inverness
Sons of Ragnvald bt Locals

1215 Not Recorded
Moray
Farquhar MacTaggart bt Donald Ban MacWilliam & Kenneth MacHeth

1217 (20 May) Lincoln
Lincs
Earl of Pembroke bt Louis VIII, Comte de la Perche

1235 Not Recorded
Galloway
Alexander II, King of the Scots bt Thomas of Galloway

1240 Embo
Sutherland
Earl of Sutherland bt Danes

1249 Isle of Kerrera
Argyll
? bt Alexander II, King of the Scots

1257 Y Cymerau
nr Llandeilo, Carms
Llewellyn of Gwynedd bt Henry III, King of England (forces)

Battle List

1261 Not Recorded
Hebrides
Earl of Ross bt Norse

1262 Caithness/Isles of Lewis & Skye
Haakon IV, King of Norway bt locals in a series of encounters

1262 Maelienydd
Area sw Dolforwyn, Radnors
Llewellyn of Gwynedd bt Roger Mortimer

1263 Blorenge Mountain
2^1/$_2$m sw Abergavenny, Glam
Llewellyn of Gwynedd bt Lords Brecon & Abergavenny

1263 (2 Oct) Largs
Ayrs
Alexander III, King of the Scots (forces) bt Haakon IV, King of Norway

1264(14 May) Lewes
Offham Hill, Lewes, Sussex
Simon de Montfort, Earl of Leicester bt Prince (Lord) Edward & Henry III, King of England

1265 (4 Aug) Evesham
Battle Well, Green Hill, Evesham
(65 yds s B4084/40 yds w A435)
Prince (Lord) Edward bt Simon de Montfort, Earl of Leicester

1271 Caerphilly
Glam
Llewellyn of Gwynedd bt Baron Gilbert de Clare

1282 (16 Jun) nr Dinefwr
Llandeilo, Carms
Llewellyn of Gwynedd bt Baron Gilbert de Clare

1282 (6 Nov) Menai Straits
Caerns
Llewellyn of Gwynedd bt Luc de Tany

1282 (11 Dec) Orewyn Bridge
Confluence of Rivers Wye & Edw, 3^1/$_2$m se Builth Wells, Brecknock
Edward I, King of England bt Llewellyn of Gwynedd

1283 (25 Apr) Bere Castle
Merioneth
English bt Welsh

1294 String of Lorn,
Argyll (exact location not known)
MacDougalls bt Campbells

1295 (5 Mar) Maes Maidog(Moydog)
1m n Castle Careinion, Monts
Earl of Warwick bt Madog ap Llewellyn

1296 Loudon Hill
2m e Darvel, Ayrs
William Wallace bt English

1296 (30 Mar) Berwick
Northumberland
Edward I, King of England bt Scottish Nobles (Sir Wm Douglas)

1296 Stracathro
n Brechin, Angus
Edward I, King of England bt John Balliol, King of the Scots

Battle List

1296 (23/27 Apr) Spottismuir
Dunbar, East Lothian
Edward I, King of England & Earl of
Surrey bt and deposed John Balliol,
King of the Scots

1297 Sanquhar
Dumfries
Sir Wm Douglas bt English

1297 Dalswinton
6m n Dumfries
William Wallace bt English

1297 (10 Aug) Lochmaben
Dumfries
Henry Percy bt Scots

1297 (11 Sep) Stirling Bridge
Stirlings
William Wallace bt Earl of Surrey &
Cressingham

1298 (22 Jul) Falkirk
Stirlings, s of Callender Wood?
Edward I, King of England bt
Sir William Wallace

1300/2 River Cree
nr Newton Stewart, Wigtowns
Edward I, King of England bt
Buchan, Comyn, & Umfreville

1303 (24 Feb) Roslin
s Edinburgh
John Comyn & Simon Fraser bt
John Segrove & Ralph de Manton

1303 (May) Stirling
Stirlings
Edward I, King of England bt Scots
(Sir John Comyn)

1304 (Feb) Happrew
w Lauder, Midlothian
Edward I, King of England bt Sir
William Wallace

1304 (Sep) Black Earnside or
Ironside
Between Abernethy and Lindores,
Fife
Sir William Wallace v Sir Aymer de
Valence. Result undecided

1306 (19 June) Methven Park
6m nw Perth, Perths
Earl of Pembroke bt Robert Bruce,
King of the Scots

1306 (13 Jul/11/23 Aug) Dalrigh
1m se Tyndrum, Stirlings
John MacDougall of Argyll, Lord of
Lorne bt Robert Bruce, King of the
Scots

1307 Turnberry
Ayrs
Robert Bruce, King of the Scots bt
Earl of Pembroke

1307 (9 Feb) Loch Ryan
Stranraer, Wigtowns
Dugald Macdowell bt Thomas &
Alexander Bruce

1307 (Mar/Apr/Sep) Glentrool
n Wigtown, Wigtowns
Robert Bruce, King of the Scots bt
Earl of Pembroke

1307 (8 May) Sanquhar
Dumfries
Sir James (The Black) Douglas bt
English

Battle List

1307 (10 May) Loudon Hill
2m e Darvel, Ayrs
Robert Bruce, King of the Scots bt
Earl of Pembroke

1307 (13 May) Ayr
Ayrs
Robert Bruce, King of the Scots bt
Ralph de Monthermet

1307 Fail
1½m nw Tarbolton, Ayrs
Not Recorded

1307 (14 Sep) Paisley Forest
Renfrews
English bt Scots

1307 (Dec) Huntly/Slioch
2m se Huntly, Aberdeens
Robert Bruce, King of the Scots v
Earl of Buchan (inconclusive)

1307/8 (winter) Inverurie
Aberdeens
Robert Bruce, King of the Scots bt
Earl of Buchan

1308 (23 May) Barra Hill
ne Inverurie/sw Old Meldrum,
Aberdeens
Robert Bruce, King of the Scots bt
Earl of Buchan

1308 Aikey Brae
1m w New Deer, Aberdeens
Robert Bruce, King of the Scots bt
Earl of Buchan

1308 (29 Jun) River Dee
Kirkcudbrights
Edward Bruce, King of the Scots bt
English (Roland)

1308 Kirroughtree
2m e Newton Stewart, Wigtowns
Edward Bruce, King of the Scots bt
English (John de St John)

1308 Brander Pass
Argyll
Robert Bruce, King of the Scots bt
MacDougalls

1311 Corbridge
Northumberland
Robert Bruce, King of the Scots bt
English

1311 Berwick
Northumberland
English bt Robert Bruce, King of the
Scots

1311 Linlithgow
West Lothian
Robert Bruce, King of the Scots bt
English

1312 Hexham
Northumberland
Robert Bruce, King of the Scots bt
English

1312 Durham
Co. Durham
Robert Bruce, King of the Scots bt
English

1312 Hartlepool
Co,Durham
James Douglas bt English

1313 Edinburgh
Midlothian
Robert Bruce, King of the Scots bt
English

Battle List

1313 Roxburgh Castle
Roxburghs
Robert Bruce, King of the Scots bt
English

1313 Perth
Perths
Robert Bruce, King of the Scots bt
English

1314 (14 Mar) Edinburgh
Midlothian
Earl of Moray bt English Garrison

1314 (23 Jun) Bannockburn
2m s Stirling, Stirlings
Robert Bruce, King of the Scots bt
Edward II, King of England

1315 Fordell
Fife
William Sinclair, Bishop of Dunkeld
bt English

1316 (Feb) Skaithmuir
nr Coldstream, Berwicks
Sir James Douglas bt Berwick
Raiders

1317(Mar/Sep?) Lintalee/Linthaughlee
Jedburgh,Roxburghs
Sir James Douglas bt Earl of Arundel

1317 (Jun?) nr Berwick
Northumberland
Sir James Douglas bt Robert
Neville of Raby

1317/8 Donibristle
Fife
Bishop of Dunkeld bt English

1318 (Apr) Berwick
Northumberland
Robert Bruce, King of the Scots
(forces) bt Edward II, King of
England (forces)

1319 (20 Sep) Mytton/Myton in
Swaledale ("The White Battle" &
"The Chapter of Mytton")
Yorks
Sir James Douglas bt Archbishop
Melton

1319 Gasklune
Angus
Duncansons bt Walter Ogilvy

1322 (16 Mar) Boroughbridge
Yorks
Sir Andrew Harclay bt Earl of
Lancaster

1322 (14 Oct) Byland
ne Malton, Yorks
Robert Bruce, King of the Scots
(forces) bt Edward II, King of
England

1332 (9 Aug) Dupplin Moor
nr Perth, Perths
Edward Balliol bt Earl of Mar

1333 (19 Jul) Halidon Hill
3m nw Berwick, Northumberland
Edward III, King of England bt
Archibald Douglas

1335 Borough Muir
Edinburgh, Midlothian
Earl of Moray bt Guy, Count of
Namur

Battle List

1335 (30 Nov) Culblean
2½m nw Dinnet, Aberdeens
Sir Andrew Moray bt David of
Strathbogie

1339 Dunbar
East Lothian
Agnes, Countess of March bt Earl
of Salisbury

1346 (13/17 Oct) Neville's Cross
1m nw Durham on A167
Ralph Neville, Earl of Westmorland
bt David II, King of the Scots

1347 Not Recorded
Roxburghs
English bt Scots

1355 Nisbet on Teviot
Roxburghs
Scots bt English

1370 Carham on Tweed
nw Wark, Northumberland
Sir John Gordon bt Sir John Lilburn

1377 (June) Rye
Sussex
French & Castillians commanded by
Jean de Vienne bt Locals

1380 Solway
English/Scottish Border
Scots bt English

1381 (Jun?) North Walsham
4m sse North Walsham, Norfolk
Bishop Despenser bt Locals

c1384 Bealligh-na-Broig
nr Balnagown, Ross
Earl Ross bt Clans "Iver, Talvich,
and Laiwe"

1387 (20Dec) Radcot Bridge
e Lechlade, Oxon
Earls of Derby & Gloucester bt Earl
of Oxford

1388 (19 Aug) Otterburn/Chevy
Chase
Northumberland. 1m nw of village &
n of A696
James, Earl of Douglas bt Sir Ralph
& Henry Percy

1392 (Aug) Glasclune
2m nw Blairgowrie, Perths
Alexander Stewart of Badenoch bt ?

1395 Tuttim-Turwigh
Strathnaver, Sutherland
MacKays bt Malcolm MacLeod

1396 North Inch, Perth
Perths
Chattans & Kays fought to the
death

1400 (Jan) Maidenhead,
Berks
Henry IV, King of England bt Earl of Kent

1400 (Jan) Cirencester,
Glos
Henry IV, King of England bt Earls
of Kent & Salisbury

1400 (Mar) Cockburnspath
East Lothian
Eldest son of Earl of Douglas bt
Henry Percy

Battle List

1400 (Sep/Oct) Fulhope Law
8m ene Carter Bar, Northumberland
Sir Ralph Umfraville bt Scots

1400 (24 Sep) Welshpool
Monts
Henry Burnell bt Owen Glendower

1401 (Jun) Hyddgen
On slopes of Plynlimon 7m sse
Machynlleth, Monts
Owen Glendower bt Henry IV, King
of England (forces)

1402 (31 Jan) Ruthin
Denbighs
Owen Glendower bt Reginald Grey,
Lord of Ruthin

1402 (22 Jun) Pilleth/Bryn Glas
2m nw Whitton, Radnors on B4356
Owen Glendower bt Henry IV, King
of England (forces under Edward
Mortimer)

1402 (22 Jun) Nesbit Moor
5m n Wooler, Northumberland
English bt Scots

1402 (14 Sep) Homildon Hill
now Humbleton Hill $1^1/4$m nw
Wooler, Northumberland
Henry Percy, Earl of Northumberland
bt Archibald, Earl of Douglas

1403 (21 Jul) Shrewsbury
Battlefield, 5m ne Shrewsbury,
Salop
Henry IV, King of England bt Henry
Percy, Earl of Northumberland

1403 (Jul) Laugharne
Pembrokes
Lord Thomas Carew bt Owen
Glendower

1403 (Nov) Caernarvon
Caerns
Jean d'Espagne bt English

1404 (Jan) Beaumaris
Anglesey
French bt English

1404 (Jan/Jun) Aberystwyth
Cardigans
Owen Glendower bt English

1404 (Jan/Jun) Harlech
Merioneth
Owen Glendower bt English

1404 Campstone Hill
3m sw Grosmont Castle, Mons
Earl of Warwick bt Owen
Glendower

1405 Craig y Dorth
se Abergavenny, Mons
Henry IV, King of England (forces)
bt Owen Glendower

1405 (11 Mar) Grosmont,
Mons
Prince Henry (later Henry V) bt
Owen Glendower (forces under
Rhys Gethin)

1405 (5 May) Pwllmelyn
nr Usk, Mons
Henry IV, King of England (forces)
bt Owen Glendower

Battle List

1405 (29 May) Skipton Moor,
Yorks
Henry IV, King of England bt
Richard Scrope, Archbishop of York

1405 (Aug) Worcester/Woodbury
Hill
Worcs
Henry IV, King of England bt Owen
Glendower

1405 (10 Aug) Haverfordwest
Pembs
French bt English

1405 (Aug) Tenby
Pembs
English bt French

1405 (Aug) Carmarthen,
Carms
French bt English

1408 (19 Feb) Bramham Moor
w Tadcaster, Yorks
Sheriff of Yorkshire bt Earl of
Northumberland & Thomas Bardolf

1408 (Sep) Aberystwyth
Cardigans
Prince Henry bt Owen Glendower

1409 (Mar) Harlech
Merioneth
Prince Henry bt Owen Glendower

1411 Dingwall
Ross
Donald MacDonald, Lord of the
Isles bt MacKays

1411 (24 Jul) Pitcaple/Harlaw
3m se Pitcaple, Aberdeens
Donald MacDonald, Lord of the
Isles v Alexander Stewart, Earl of
Mar. Indecisive

1424 Dumbarton
Dunbartons
Lord James Stewart bt James I,
King of the Scots (forces)

1426 Harpsdale
nr Spittal, Caithness
Gunns v Mackays (inconclusive)

1427 Strathnaver
Sutherland
Angus Dow bt Angus of Moray

1431 Druim na Coub
Tongue, Sutherland
Angus Dubh (forces) bt Morgan &
Neil Mowat

1431 Inverlochy
1m n Fort William, Inverness
Highlanders bt Earls of Mar &
Caithness

1435 (10 Sep) Piper Dene
2m s Wark, Northumberland
Earl of Angus bt Earl of
Northumberland & Sir Robert Ogle

1437 "The Chase of Sandside"
Reay, Caithness
Mackays bt Men of Caithness

1438 Tannack Moor
nr Wick, Caithness
Keiths & Mackays bt Gunns

Battle List

1445 Arbroath
Angus
Lindsays bt Ogilvies

1448 (23 Oct) Gretna/River Sark
Dumfries
Hugh Douglas, Earl of Ormonde bt
Earl of Northumberland

1450 (18 Jun) Sevenoaks
Kent
Jack Cade bt Sir Humphrey Stafford

1450 (5 Jul) Southwark
Surrey
Jack Cade bt Matthew Gough

1452 (18 May) Brechin
Hillhead, 2m nw Brechin, Angus
Earl of Huntly bt Earl of Crawford

1453 Stamford Bridge
Yorks
Sir Thomas Neville v Lord
Egremont. Result not recorded

1455 (12 May) Arkinholm
Erkinholme on R Esk s Langholm,
Dumfries
Earl of Angus bt Earl Douglas

1455 (22 May) St Albans
Herts
Richard of York bt Henry VI, King of
England

1459 (23 Sep) Blore Heath
2¹/₂m e Market Drayton, Salop
Earl of Salisbury bt Lord Audley

1459 (12 Oct) Ludford Bridge
Ludlow, Salop
Henry VI, King of England bt
Richard of York

1460 (10 Jul) Northampton
Northants
Earl of Warwick bt Henry VI, King of
England

1460 (Aug) Roxburgh
Roxburghs
James II, King of the Scots bt
English

1460 (16 Dec) Worksop
Notts
Lancastrians bt Richard of York

1460 (30 Dec) Wakefield
Sandal, 2m s Wakefield, Yorks
Duke of Somerset bt Richard of
York

1461 (2 Feb) Mortimer's Cross
4m e Presteigne, Herefords
Edward of York bt Earls of Wilts &
Pembrokes

1461 Dunstable
Beds
Queen Margaret bt Yorkists

1461 (17 Feb) St Albans
Herts
Queen Margaret bt Earl of Warwick

1461 (28 Mar) Ferrybridge
Yorks
Lord Clifford bt Lord FitzWalter

Battle List

1461 (28 Mar) Dintingdale
between Saxton village & A162
Tadcaster-Ferrybridge road, Yorks
Lord Fauconberg bt Lord Clifford

1461 (29 Mar) Towton
6m n Ferrybridge, Yorks, between
Towton & Saxton villages
Edward IV, King of England bt Duke
of Somerset

1464 (25 Apr) Hedgeley Moor
Wooperton, 6m se Wooler,
Northumberland
Marquess of Montague bt Sir Ralph
Percy & Duke of Somerset

1464 (15 May) Hexham
Hexham Levels, 2m se Hexham,
Northumberland
Marquess of Montague bt Duke of
Somerset

1464 (Jun) Bamburgh Castle
Northumberland
Earl of Warwick bt Sir Ralph Grey

1469 (26 Jul) Edgecote
6m ne Banbury, Oxon
Sir John Conyers bt Earl of
Pembroke

1470 (12 Mar) Losecoat Field
3m ne Empingham, Rutlands
Edward IV, King of England bt Sir
Robert Welles

1471 (3 Apr) Leicester,
Leics
Edward IV, King of England bt
Lancastrians

1471 (14 Apr) Barnet
Hadley Highstone, Herts
Edward IV, King of England bt Earl
of Warwick

1471 (4 May) Tewkesbury
Glos
Edward IV, King of England bt
Queen Margaret (Duke of Somerset
commanded)

1480 Lagebread
W Ross
Angus Ross bt MacKenzies

1480 "Bloody Bay"
nr Tobermory, Mull, Argyll
Angus MacDonald (forces) bt Lord
of the Isles (forces)

1484 (22 Jul) Kirkconnel
Dumfries
Locals bt Duke of Albany

1485 (22 Aug) Bosworth Field
2m s Market Bosworth, Leics
Henry VII (Tudor) bt Richard III,
King of England

1487 Aldy-Charrish
W Ross
MacKays bt Rosses

1487 (16 Jun) Stoke Field
East Stoke, 3m s Newark, Notts
Henry VII, King of England bt Earl
of Lincoln

1488 Talla Moss (Rout of)
Between Stirling & Forth, Stirlings
Locals bt Earl of Lennox

Battle List

1488 (11 Jun) Sauchieburn
s Stirling, Stirlings
James, Duke of Rothesay bt James
III, King of the Scots

1491 Blair na Parc
Strathconon, Ross
MacKenzies bt Alexander of
Lochalsh

1497 (17 Jun) Blackheath
Kent
Henry VII, King of England bt
James Touchet, Baron Audley

1497 (Jul) Norham
Northumberland
Earl of Surrey bt James IV, King of
the Scots

1497 (17-18 Sep) Exeter
Devon
Earl of Devonshire bt Perkin
Warbeck

1513 Milfield ("The Ill Raid")
se Coldstream, Berwicks
Sir William Bulmer bt Lord Home

1513 (28 Aug) Norham
Northumberland
James IV, King of the Scots bt
Bishop of Durham

1513 (9 Sep) Flodden
se Branxton, Northumberland
Earl of Surrey bt James IV, King of
the Scots

1514 Hornshole
3m e Hawick, Roxburghs
Local Youths bt Marauding English
soldiers from Hexham

1515 Edinburgh ("Cleanse the
Causeway")
Midlothian
Earl of Angus bt Sir Patrick
Hamilton

1516 Torran-Dubh
nr Rogart, Sutherland
Alexander Sutherland bt John
MacKay

1518 Craiganairgid
Creag an Airgid 2m nw Kilchoan,
Argyll
Sir Donald of Lochalsh & Alexander
of Islay bt Maclan of Ardnamurchan

1520 Edinburgh
Midlothian
Douglas bt Earl of Arran

1529 Summerdale
Orkney
? bt Earl John

1542 (Aug) Hadden Rigg
Teviotdale, Roxburghs
Earl of Huntly bt Sir Robert Bowes
& Earl of Angus

1542 (24 Nov) Solway Moss
2m ne Gretna, Dumfries
Sir Oliver Sinclair & Lord Wharton
bt James V, King of the Scots

1544 (3 Jul) Invergarry ("Battle of
the Shirts"/"Blar na leine")
2m sw Invergarry at s end Loch Oich,
Inverness
Clans Ranald, Cameron, and Donald
(8/700 survived) claimed victory over
Clan Fraser (4/400 survived)!

Battle List

1545 (12/17/25 Feb) Ancrum Moor
se St Boswells, Roxburghs
Earl of Angus bt Sir Ralph Evers &
Sir Brian Layton

1547 (21 Jul) St Andrews
Fife
Leo Strozzi bt "Castilians"

1547 (10 Sep) Pinkie Cleugh
s Musselburgh, E Lothian
Duke of Somerset bt Earls of Arran
& Huntly

1549 (4 Aug) Fenny Bridges
Honiton, Devon
Lord Russell bt Earl of Arundel

1549 (17 Aug) Sampford Courtney
Devon
Lord Russell bt Earl of Arundel

1549 (26 Aug) Dussindale
Norwich, Norfolk
Earl of Warwick bt Robert Kett

1554 (Jan/Mar) Wrotham
Kent
Lord Abergavenny bt Sir Henry Islay

1554 (Feb/Mar) Cooling Castle
5m ne Rochester, Kent
Sir Thomas Wyatt bt Royalists

1554 (Feb/Mar) Cobham
Kent
Sir Thomas Wyatt bt Royalists

1556 Ben Mor
Berriedale, Caithness
Sutherlands bt MacKays

1562 Skirmish Hill
Darnick, Roxburghs
Clan Scott bt Clan Douglas

1562 (28 Oct) Corrichie Hill
5m n Banchory, Aberdeens
Earl of Moray bt Earl of Huntly

1567 (15 Jun) Carberry Hill
s Musselburgh, E Lothian
Earl of Moray bt Earl of Bothwell

1568 (13 May) Langside
Glasgow, Lanarks
Earl of Moray bt Earl of Argyll

1570 The Gelt
13 m se Carlisle, Cumberland
Lord Hunsdon bt Leonard Dacre

1571 (10 Oct) Tillyangus
2m sw Clatt, Aberdeens
Gordons bt Forbes

1571 (20 Nov) Crabstane
nr junct. Hardgate & Justice Mills
Lane s of w end Union St
Aberdeen, Aberdeens
Gordons bt Forbes

1575 Carter Bar ("Raid of the
Reidswire")
Roxburghs/Northumberland border
Sir John Carmichael bt Sir John Forster

1586 Aldgown
Not Recorded, probably Caithness
Gunns and MacKays bt Sinclairs

1589 Clyne
2m nw Brora, Sutherland
Men of Sutherland v Men of
Caithness (Inconclusive)

Battle List

1593 (Dec) Dryfe Sands
Lockerbie, Dumfries
Johnstones, Elliotts, Scotts, Irvines
& Grahams bt Maxwells &
Armstrongs

1594 (4 Oct)Glenlivet/Alltacoileachan
at the head of Glen Rinnes, Moray
Earl of Huntly bt Earl of Argyll

1598 (5 Aug) Traigh Gruinart
Isle of Islay, Argyll
Sir James MacDonald of Islay bt Sir
Lachlan MacLean of Duart

1599 Leckmelm
Ross
Earl of Sutherland bt Gunns

1600 (5 Aug) Perth
Gowrie House
James VI, King of the Scots bt Earl
of Gowrie

1601 Benquihillin
Isle of Skye, Inverness
MacDonalds bt MacLeods

1601 Carinish
N Uist, Inverness
Donald MacDonald of Eriskay bt
MacLeods

1603 Luss ("Slaughter of Lennox")
Dunbs
MacGregors bt Buchanans

1603 (Feb) Glenfruin
Dunbs
Alasdair MacGregor of Glenstrae bt
Colquhoun of Luss

1639 (14 Feb) Turriff
Aberdeens
Marquis of Huntly v Covenanters.
Inconclusive

1639 (14 May) Turriff ("The Trot of
Turriff")
Aberdeens
Lt Col William Johnston, Sir George
Ogilvy & Sir John Gordon bt
Covenanters

1639 (15 Jun) Megray Hill
n Stonehaven, Kincardines
Covenanters bt Col William Gunn

1639 (18 Jun) Brig o'Dee
Aberdeens
Earl of Montrose bt Col William
Gunn

1640 (28 Aug) Newburn
6m w Newcastle, Northumberland
Alexander Leslie bt Lord Conway

1642 (23 Sep) Powick Bridge
Worcester
Prince Rupert bt Col John Brown &
Earl of Essex

1642 (23 Oct) Edgehill
Warks. Between B4086 Kineton-
Warmington & A422 Stratford-
Banbury
Prince Rupert v Earl of Essex.
Inconclusive

1642 (12 Nov) Brentford
Middx
Lord Forth & Prince Rupert bt Col
Holles

Battle List

1642 (1 Dec) Piercebridge
Co Durham
Earl of Newcastle bt Roundheads

1642 (6 Dec) Tadcaster
Yorks
Earl of Newcastle bt Lord Fairfax

1643 (19 Jan) Bra(d)dock Down
4m ne Lostwithiel, Cornwall
Sir Bevil Grenville & Sir Ralph
Hopton bt Earl of Stamford

1643 (2-4 Mar) Lichfield
Staffs
Roundheads (Lord Brooke) bt
Royalists

1643 (19 Mar) Hopton Heath
2m ne Stafford, Staffs
Lord Hastings & Earl of
Northampton bt Sir John Gell

1643 (24 Mar) Highnam
Glos
Sir William Waller bt Lord Herbert

1643 (30 Mar) Seacroft Moor
ne Leeds,Yorks
Royalists bt Lord Fairfax

1643 (22 Apr) Launceston
Cornwall
Sir Ralph Hopton bt James
Chudleigh

1643 (25 Apr) Sourton Down
3m sw Okehampton, Devon
James Chudleigh bt Sir Ralph
Hopton

1643 (26 Apr) Reading
Berks
Earl of Essex bt Royalists

1643 (13 May) Grantham
Lincs
Oliver Cromwell bt Royalists

1643 (16 May) Stratton
1m e Bude, Cornwall
Sir Ralph Hopton bt James
Chudleigh

1643 (May) Sleaford
Lincs
Earl of Newcastle bt Oliver
Cromwell

1643 (12 Jun) Chewton Mendip
4m wsw Midsomer Norton,
Somerset
Sir William Waller v Sir Ralph
Hopton. Inconclusive

1643 (18 Jun) Chalgrove
w Chalgrove-Warpsgrove road
Oxon
Prince Rupert bt Col John
Hampden

1643 (30 Jun) Atherton/Adwalton
Moor
5m se Bradford, Yorks
Earl of Newcastle bt Lord Fairfax &
Sir Thomas Fairfax

1643 (5 Jul) Lansdown
4m n Bath, Somerset
Sir Ralph Hopton bt Sir William
Waller

Battle List

1643 (13 Jul) Roundway Down
n Devizes, Wilts
Sir Ralph Hopton bt Sir William
Waller

1643 (26 Jul) Bristol
Glos
Prince Rupert bt Nathaniel Fiennes,
Joan Batten & Dorothy Hazzard

1643 (28 Jul) Gainsborough
Lincs
Oliver Cromwell bt Royalists

1643 (28 Aug) Torrington
5m se Bideford, Devon
Sir John Digby bt Local levies

1643 (18 Sep) Aldbourne Chase
Between Aldbourne & Chiseldon,
Wilts
Earl of Essex v Prince Rupert.
Inconclusive

1643 (20 Sep) Newbury
Berks, s of town
Earl of Essex v Prince Rupert.
Inconclusive

1643 (11 Oct) Winceby
e Horncastle, Lincs at junction of
A158/A1115
Oliver Cromwell bt Sir John
Henderson

1643 (11 Oct) Hull
Yorks
Lord Fairfax v Earl of Newcastle.
Inconclusive

1644 (25 Jan) Nantwich
Cheshire
Sir Thomas Fairfax bt Lord Byron

1644 (Jan) Howden Hills
Yorks
Earl of Newcastle bt Lord Leven

1644 (6 Mar) Muskham Bridge
1¹/₂m nw Newark, Notts
Sir John Meldrum bt Col Holles

1644 (22 Mar) Newark
Notts
Prince Rupert bt Sir John Meldrum

1644 (25 Mar) Bradford
Yorks
John Lambert bt Maj Gen George
Porter & John Belasyse (Lord
Bellasis)

1644 (29 Mar) Cheriton Wood
Hants e of village
Sir William Waller bt Baron (Sir
Ralph) Hopton

1644 (11 Apr) Selby
Yorks
Sir Thomas Fairfax bt John
Belasyse (Lord Bellasis)

1644 (29 Jun) Cropredy Bridge
Oxon
Charles I, King of England,
Scotland and Ireland bt Sir William
Waller

1644 (2 Jul) Marston Moor
6m w York, between Tockwith &
Long Marston villages
Alexander Leslie, Earl of Leven bt
Prince Rupert & Lord Goring

Battle List

1644 (31 Aug) Lostwithiel
Cornwall
Charles I, King of England,
Scotland and Ireland bt Earl of
Essex

1644 (1 Sep) Tippermuir
3m w Perth, Perths
Marquess of Montrose bt Lord
Elcho

1644 (2 Sep) between Lostwithiel /
Fowey, Cornwall
Lord Goring bt Earl of Essex

1644 (13 Sep)) Justice Mills
s of w end of Union St, Aberdeen,
Aberdeens
Marquess of Montrose bt Lord
Balfour of Burleigh

1644 (18 Sep/14 Oct) Montgomery
Monts
Maj Gen Thomas Myddelton bt Lord
Byron & Irish & Welsh

1644 (27 Oct) Newbury
Berks
Charles I, King of England,
Scotland and Ireland v Sir William
Waller & Earls of Essex &
Manchester. Inconclusive

1644 (28 Oct) Fyvie
1m nnw Fyvie, Aberdeens
Marquess of Montrose bt Earl of Argyll

1644 (4 Dec) Abbeycwmhir
Radnors
Maj Gen Thomas Myddelton bt
Royalist Garrison

1645 (2 Feb) Inverlochy
n Fort William, Inverness
Marquess of Montrose bt Earl of
Argyll

1645 (4 Apr) Dundee
Angus
Lt Col John Hurry bt Marquess of
Montrose

1645 (9 May) Auldearn
2m e Nairn, Nairns
Marquess of Montrose bt Sir John
Hurry

1645 (31 May) Leicester
Leics
Lord Loughborough bt Locals

1645 (14 Jun) Naseby
Northants
Sir Thomas Fairfax bt Charles I,
King of England, Scotland and
Ireland

1645 (2 Jul) Alford
Junction A944/A980 2m w village,
Aberdeens
Marquess of Montrose bt Gen
Baillie

1645 (10 Jul) Langport
Somerset. 1000 yds e Langport on
B3153 to Somerton
Sir Thomas Fairfax bt Lord Goring

1645 (28 Jul) Dunkeld
Perths
Marquess of Montrose bt Gen
Baillie

Battle List

1645 (1 Aug) Colby Moor
Haverfordwest, Pembrokes
Col Rowland Laugharne bt Charles
Gerrard

1645 (15 Aug) Kilsyth
Stirlings
Marquess of Montrose bt Gen
Baillie

1645 (10 Sep) Bristol,
Glos
Sir Thomas Fairfax bt Prince Rupert

1645 (13 Sep) Philiphaugh
3m sw Selkirk, Selkirks
David Leslie bt Marquess of
Montrose

1645 (23 Sep) Rowton Heath
2m se Chester, Cheshire
Gen Sydenham Pointz & Col
Michael Jones bt Sir Marmaduke
Langdale

1645 (1 Nov) Denbigh
Denbighs
Sir William Brereton & Col Michael
Jones bt Sir William Vaughan

1646 (16 Feb) Torrington
5m se Bideford, Devon
Lord Hopton bt Lord Fairfax

1646 (21 Mar) Stow on the Wold
Glos
Roundheads bt Sir Jacob Astley

1647 Dunaverty
1m s Southend, Kintyre, Argyll
Earl of Argyll (forces) bt Royalists

1647 (24 May) Rhunahaorine Point
3m n Tayinloan, Kintyre, Argyll
David Leslie bt Alasdair MacColl

1648 (8 May) St Fagans
3m w Cardiff, Glam
Col Thomas Horton bt Col Rowland
Laugharne

1648 (1 Jun) Maidstone
Kent
Lord Fairfax bt Lord Norwich

1648 (5 Jun) Y Dalar Hir
Caerns
Thomas Mytton bt Sir Thomas
Owen

1648 (12 Jun) Mauchline Moor
$1\frac{1}{2}$m sw Mauchline, Ayrs
Maj Gen John Middleton & Earl of
Callender bt Anti-engagers

1648 (Jul) Colchester
Essex
Sir Thomas Fairfax bt Royalists

1648 (17-18 Aug) Preston
from Ribbleton Moor 2m ne
Preston, to Winwick, 9m ne
Warrington, Lancs
Oliver Cromwell bt Duke of
Hamilton

1648 (1 Oct) Not Recorded
Anglesey
Sir Thomas Myddleton bt Sir
Richard Bulkeley

1650 (27 Apr) Carbisdale
s Spinningdale, E Ross
Col Strachan bt Marquess of
Montrose

Battle List

1650 (19 Jul) Edinburgh
Midlothian
David Leslie bt Oliver Cromwell

1650 (3 Sep) Dunbar
East Lothian
Oliver Cromwell bt David Leslie

1651 (20 Jul) Pitreavie
nr Inverkeithing, Fife
Gen Lambert bt David Leslie

1651 (1 Sep) Dundee
Angus
Gen Monck bt Locals

1651 (3 Sep) Worcester
Worcs
Oliver Cromwell bt Charles II, King
of England, Scotland and Ireland

1652 (19 May) off Dover
Kent
Admiral Blake bt Admiral van Tromp

1652 (29 Nov) off Dungeness,
Kent
Admiral van Tromp bt Admiral Blake

1653 Aberfoyle
Perths
Earl of Glencairn bt Col Kidd

1653 (3 Jan) off North Foreland
Kent
Admiral Blake bt Admiral van Tromp

1653 (18-20 Feb) off Portland
Dorset
Admirals Blake, Deane & Monck bt
Admirals van Tromp, de Ruyter &
Evetzen

1654 Pass of Ballater
Aberdeens
Camerons & Farquharsons bt Col
Morgan

1654 (26 Jul) Loch Garry
Perths
Col Morgan bt Gen Middleton

1655 Dalnaspidal
Perths
Gen Monck bt Earl of Glencairn

1659 (Aug) Winnington Bridge
Cheshire
John Lambert bt Sir George Booth

1665 (3 Jul) off Lowestoft
Suffolk
English Navy bt Dutch Navy

1666 (1-3 Jun) "The Downs"
Off Kent
Duke of Albemarle v Admirals de
Ruyter, van Tromp & de Witt.
Inconclusive

1666 (1 Jul) The Goodwins
Off Kent
Duke of Albemarle v Admirals de
Ruyter & van Tromp. Inconclusive

1666 (25 Jul/4 Aug) North Foreland
Off Kent
Duke of Albemarle bt Admirals van
Tromp & de Ruyter

Battle List

1666 (28 Nov) Rullion Green
("Battle of the Pentlands")
Silverburn, sw Edinburgh,
Midlothian
Sir Thomas Dalziel bt Col Wallace

1672 (28 May) Southwold Bay
Suffolk
English Navy v Dutch Navy.
Inconclusive

1679 (11 Jun) Drumclog
3m e Darvel, Ayrs
Robert Hamilton & William Cleland
bt Capt John Graham of
Claverhouse

1679 (22 Jun) Bothwell Bridge
(Hamilton Moor)
7m se Glasgow, Lanarks
Duke of Hamilton bt Covenanters
led by William Cleland

1680 (20 Jul) Airds Moss
4m ne Auchinleck, Ayrs
Bruce of Earlshall bt David
Hackston of Rathillet

1680 Altimorlich
Rivulet, 4m from mouth of R Wick,
Caithness
George Sinclair, Earl of Caithness
bt Sinclair of Keiss

1685 (Jun) Keynsham
Somerset
James II, King of England, Scotland
and Ireland (forces) bt Duke of
Monmouth

1685 (Jun) Philips Norton
Norton St Philip, Somerset
James II, King of England, Scotland
and Ireland (forces) bt Duke of
Monmouth

1685 (6 Jul) Sedgemoor
3m se Bridgewater, Somerset
Earl of Feversham & John Churchill
bt Duke of Monmouth

1688 (4 Aug) Roy Bridge
Inverness
Clan MacDonell of Keppoch bt Clan
MacIntosh

1689 (27 Jul) Killiecrankie
Perths
John Graham, Viscount Dundee bt
Maj Gen Hugh MacKay

1689 (21 Aug) Dunkeld
Perths
Lt Col Wiliam Cleland bt Col
Cannon

1690 (1 May) Cromdale
Moray
Sir Thomas Livingstone bt Buchan

1692 (13 Feb) Glencoe
Argyll
Capt Robert Campbell of Glenlyon
bt MacDonalds

1715 (12 Nov) Preston
Lancs
Gen Wills & Gen Carpenter bt
Thomas Forster

Battle List

1715 (13 Nov) Sherriffmuir
2m nw Dunblane, Perths
Duke of Argyll bt Earl of Mar

1719 (10 Jun) Glenshiel
On A87 4m se Shiel Bridge W Ross
Gen Wightman bt Marquess of
Tullibardine

1745 Moy,
Inverness
MacIntoshes bt Loudon's Highlanders

1745 (2 Feb) Inverlochy
1m n Fort William, Inverness
Earl of Montrose bt Campbells

1745 (21 Sep) Prestonpans
n Tranent, E Lothian
Prince Charles Edward Stuart bt Sir
John Cope

1745 (18 Dec) Clifton
6m s Penrith, Cumberland
Prince Charles Edward Stuart v
Duke of Cumberland. Inconclusive

1745 (23 Dec) Inverurie
Aberdeens
Gordons bt MacLeods and Munros

1746 (17 Jan) Falkirk
On B803 sw Falkirk, Stirlings
Prince Charles Edward Stuart &
Lord George Murray bt Lt Gen
Henry Hawley

1746 (16 Apr) Culloden
4m e Inverness
Duke of Cumberland bt Prince
Charles Edward Stuart

1778 (22 Apr) Whitehaven
Cumberland
Locals bt John Paul Jones

1797 (23 Feb) Fishguard
Llanwnda 2m nw Fishguard,
Pembrokes
Lord John Cawdor bt Brig Gen
William Tate

END

Index

Index

Index

Index

Index

51

Index

Index

Index

Index